From London to Enugu

One man's story of kidnap, trauma, deceit and mental health.

Edozie Ameke

ISBN: 978-1-9162843-0-2

First published 2019

PREFACE

I've worked as an Academic Mentor in Schools, Colleges, Youth Clubs and Community Centres all over London for the past 30 years. Specialising in working with some of the most difficult, disruptive and disaffected students, as well as working with gifted and talented students.

Twice in my mentoring career, I've been rated 'Outstanding by 'OFSTED', the UK Government Education Standards authority.

I wrote this book as I was motivated by family and friends to tell the story of my teenage experiences, as an inspiration to young people and adults to help them overcome challenges in life.

I believe this book will help all readers to recognise that as human beings, we can choose to turn negative into positive.

In 2008, I wrote two short plays that were performed at Stratford Circus Theatre in London.

I was a member of the team who won the "Home Office Award for Excellence in Mentoring" when I was a trainer of Mentors in East London.

I also won an Award for a Peer Mentor project I set up in a secondary school in South London in partnership with mental health organisation (MIND). The local newspaper printed the story.

I created a multi-agency partnership with the BBC and produced some short dramas and documentaries that are on the BBC VideoNation website.

Alongside Menelik Shabazz, Charles Thompson MBE and others I helped to create BlackFilm-maker Magazine and the annual International Blackfilm Festival in London.

Currently, I'm writing "The Enugu House", which is a sequel to "From London To Enugu".

ACKNOWLEDGEMENTS

Kristina Sandor – for originally asking me to tell the story

Jeanine Ameke – for interviewing me and typing up the interview which formed the foundation for the book

Sade Ameke – for passion and ehthusiasm

Scherin Barlow Massay – for proof reading and editing

My brother Chiat – for always being a support

My brother Chiduve – for writing his book within six months

My other siblings – Ifeoma, Abugu, Nnabuike – for rising above the challenges of Nigeria and our childhood and succeeding in life

My foster family – for their caring and support

Contents

MY FATHER AND MOTHER

Where my parents were from

By the time I was 18 years old, I was the oldest of 6 siblings. I lived at home with my mum and one younger brother and two younger sisters.

My parents came from a village called called Umuleri. It's maybe around 45 minutes from Onitsha the market town which was once the largest market in the whole of West Africa. Umuleri is a neighbour of Aguleri. Both towns trace their origins back to Ancient Egypt. Umuleri and Aguleri had a civil war with each other and it was devastating to both communities. I grew up being aware of that because my Nigerian parents spend a lot of time trying to brainwash me with worry and fear saying, "You don't ever eat from a person from Aguleri, they will poison you". I found those kind of stories really frustrating because all they do is perpetuate prejudice.

My mother and father had an arranged marriage. My Dad was 15 years older than my mum and his family found who they believed was the right girl for him to marry and arranged it.

My Dad's whole village had come together, raised money and sponsored his trip to London, to send him to London to study. They saw him as the person who would change everything for the village. He left Nigeria a year ahead of my mum.

My Father And Mother

My parents were immigrants to Britain from Nigeria. My father came to London in 1962 and my mother followed him a year later in 1963. They were married in a traditional Igbo marriage ceremony. When they were together in London they married again in a traditional Christian church ceremony. Nigerian Igbo marriage was not considered legitimate.

My Mum was very entrepreneurial. She created a special hair cream for black women and sold it. She also made wigs for black women. My mum and my dad used to buy cars in London, and would get strong cars from Belgium or Germany or Northern England and send them to Nigeria and make them taxis.

I was born in 1964 in London to Nigerian parents. My mother told me that in the early 1960s, before I was born, in those days getting a job was so easy that if you left your job on Thursday evening, you could start a new job on Friday morning.

My mother was an orphan long before I was born. She said that her parents and her only brother who was a priest, all died when she was young. My Dad came to London from Nigeria to study electrical engineering in 1962 or '63. Apparently he was setting up a company to provide electricity to the whole of West Africa. When I was a kid, I saw the plans and the drawings for it. He was a soldier in the Biafran war during the 60s. That was the war where the UK backed northern Nigeria to kill a million Igbo people. My people.

From 1964 to 1976, just before my Dad died, before he got sick, my mum said those were the best years of her life.

At age 12, I was visiting my father in hospital as he was dying. I always bought him grapes. Once I ate them before I got to the hospital, and said that they didn't have any grapes in the shop. But I think he knew that I'd eaten them.

I was 13 years old at the time, and the oldest of 6 siblings ranging from 13 years old to 2 years old. My mum put me and my brother Chiat to stay with my foster family, and my sisters stayed somewhere else, while my mum went to Nigeria to bury him and took Chiduve and Nnabuike, my two youngest siblings with her. After the burial, she came back to London without my two youngest siblings. She left them there in Nigeria. It was a shock to me and I didn't understand or know why she left them there.

My mother said that my father was murdered by poison. Even at that young age, I found what she said to be unhelpful and disturbing. I felt it wasn't the right kind of thing to say to say to a 13 year old, and it made me angry. I felt as though she wanted me to feel guilty and seek revenge against my father's poisoners. I really had no idea what I was supposed to do with that kind of information at that age. My mum said that people tried to take his ideas and they poisoned him because they were jealous of his potential success.

Elvis Presley and my father

Dad was strict with hard discipline. We would be beaten by a stick or belt if we did the wrong thing. My Dad would say to me, "Go and get a stick from the garden! ". I would try to get a small one, but it never worked. If it was too small my dad would go to the garden and get a bigger thicker one.

Sometimes my dad would get on all fours and me and my brother Chiat would climb on his back and pretend we were riding a horse. My Dad was an avid Guardian newspaper reader. In those days the paper was huge, about three or four feet in length. Me and my brother Chiat were serious comics readers and collectors. Those comics meant everything to us. We discussed and debated the latest superhero adventures endlessly and we had early or first editions of some of the most precious Marvel comics. My Dad felt that comics weren't good for our minds, so one day he threw away all the comics we'd collected. It was one of the cruellest things that he did.

My love of the cinema was born when my father took me and my brother to the children's weekly cinema in Clapham Junction. We called it 'saturday morning pictures'. One of my favourite movies of that time was " The Three Musketeers". After that movie all the kids came out and played in the streets outside the cinema and pretended to be one of the musketeers. D'artagnan was my favourite name for years after.

There was a very strong sense of cultural alienation growing up in London in the late 1960s and early 1970s. It was very rare to see anyone of African-Caribbean heritage in any jobs or career that was important. It made you feel that being of African-Caribbean heritage wasn't valued. In addition, the racism in the newspapers and media was fully accepted as natural and normal. Many of the TV shows made open mockery of people from cultural minorities. So it was a huge boost in morale to see black American artists, politicians, musicians and leaders making progress in getting positive representation. Even the Jackson 5 cartoon was important to us as people of African-Caribbean heritage.

My father made wonderful 'egg bread' and the best thickest chips. I thought that he was a much better cook than my mother. Sometimes he took me and my brother Chiat with him to get cheap chicken. We would see the chicken being slaughtered, and still running around even though they were headless. Afterwards my Dad would take us with him to visit one of his friends. They would talk for hours in Igbo which me and my brother didn't understand. They would leave me and Chiat in front of the TV. I remember me and Chiat having a great time watching "Jason & The Argonauts".

'Uncle Charles' / Charles Hirsch was my foster father. Patricia Hirsch was my foster mother. I used to call her 'Aunty Pat'. While he was alive, my Dad tried to teach me some Igbo in order to impress my foster father. "Ello challenkem kedu kemel tata" means, "Hello uncle Charles, how are you today?". That was the total extent of the Igbo I learned before my Dad died.

My Dad had a younger brother who lived in London. His name was Ekwelli. We hardly ever saw him. I was really sad about that. He was a very debonair playboy type. He looked like a more handsome version of Marvin Gaye. He smoked a pipe and usually wore a neck tie cravat, sort of like a scarf around his neck. He was always very fashionable.

While my father was sick and dying in Nigeria, my mother made me and my siblings do voice recordings to send to him in Nigeria. I always felt silly doing it and really hated it. We had to pretend to be extra sad or extra happy. I hated putting on fake performances. And of course, speaking into a microphone with no interaction from my father was very hard.

Seeing my Dad on a drip in hospital was weird and surreal like watching a film. He was supposed to be just a bit sick and supposed to get better soon, but I knew he was going to die. In my mind, even at that age I knew that people who were in hospital on a drip were going to die.

One day a telegram from Nigeria arrived. I was the person that saw it on the floor of in front of the letter box. I knew exactly what it said before I picked it up from the floor and opened it. In those days you rarely received a telegram unless it was extremely important, or very bad news. Inside me I knew what the telegram said. I was calm, but I knew that it would be very difficult for my mother to receive the news. For a split second I toyed with the idea of not telling her. But I knew that to delay it would only make it worse.

I'll never forget the last major hit that Elvis Presley had was a song called "Way Down". That song came out in 1977, people remember that year as the year that Elvis Presley died. I remember it as the year my father died.

As soon as I told my mother, she broke into a demonic fit of screaming and crying that I thought would never end. She was inconsolable for days, and a steady procession of family friends and relatives visited for several weeks. She became a single mother of 6 children aged 13 years old to 2 years old. She dressed all in black for a year. That drove me crazy as it was so depressing seeing her all in black for a year.

Rebel Living

I'd loved writing short stories and poems since I'd been very young. By the time I was about 15, I was writing longer stories based on the things that me and my friends used to get up to. Near where I lived was a place that empty train carriages were left overnight or for days. We used to go down there mostly during the day, but sometimes at night and pair off in couples and make out.

At the age of 15, Richard Campbell was my best friend. He was a white guy also aged 15. I turned him on to reggae. He was the first person I ever saw who had holes in the knees of his jeans. Nowadays people pay over 200 pounds for that, but his jeans were just worn out!

Around that age I used to go to a youth club called LARA. It was an acronym that stood for Louvaine Area Residents Association. In the early 70's the local council had planned to build a motorway through the area. The residents of Louvaine Rd and a few of the surrounding streets got together and formed a community action group to fight against the motorway. They were successful and set up a community centre in the name of the community group. I grew up in and lived in Louvaine Rd with my parents who were foundation members of that community group.

When I was about 16 years old, one of the Youth Workers at LARA Youth Club was a Rastaman named Greg. He was a very inspirational guy and a strong positive mentor and motivator for me and other young people. One day he took me and about 5 other young people on a weekend trip to Birmingham. He treated us in a very mature way, took us to some late -night reggae clubs and trusted us to be mature minded and responsible. He was a great inspiration in my attitude to life.

Up to the age of about 16, I used to wash all my clothes by hand. We didn't have a washing machine. Washing clothes by hand is extremely hard work, especially jeans. On rare occasions before that I would take all the family washing to the launderette. Usually on my own, and sometimes with my brother Chiat.

The Lyceum

'The Lyceum' nightclub in The Strand in central London was my absolute favourite nightclub from when I was aged 16 to 18 years old. The music was Soul and dance disco. It was a multi-culturally black and white mixed crowd. Me and my friends used to go there either on a Saturday night or Friday night. The nightclub had previously been a theatre and that added to the atmosphere on the dance floor.

Some of the crew who I used to go with or meet at the club were Jackie Molloy, who grew up on the same street as me, three young women who we called "The Soul Sisters" who were from South London, and Alan Hamilton who always wore sunglasses at night, even in the nightclub. He never ever took them off!

There was a song by 'The Gap Band' called "Oops Upside Your Head" that for some strange reason everyone sat down on the dance-floor and got into long rows and pretended they were rowing! It was the craziest dance move that I'd ever seen or known. It was a lot of fun.

One night at the Lyceum I was in the corridor outside of the dance floor with a young woman. We were being physically intimate and were caught by one of the security guards.

Initially he walked us straight outside of the building, but he relented, let us back inside the building and made us promise to never do it again. Some promises are very hard to keep.

Birthday Riots

April 13th 1981 was my birthday and I was 17 years old. It was also the second day of riots in Brixton in South London. A lot of my friends went down to Brixton and got involved in the riots and I seriously considered joining them. But I decided that I didn't want to spend my birthday rioting. I spent the day with my girlfriend Joyce.

The **1981 Brixton riot** was a confrontation between the Metropolitan Police and protesters in Brixton, South London, England, between 10 and 12 April 1981. The main riot on 11 April, resulted in almost 280 injuries to police and 45 injuries to members of the public, over a hundred vehicles were burned, including 56 police vehicles; almost 150 buildings were damaged, with thirty burned. There were 82 arrests, and up to 5,000 people were involved.

Brixton in South London was an area with serious social and economic problems. The whole United Kingdom was affected by a recession by 1981, but the local African-Caribbean community was suffering particularly high unemployment, poor housing, and a higher than average crime rate.

In the preceding months, there had been growing unease between the police and the inhabitants of Lambeth. On 18 January 1981 a number of black youths died in a fire during a house party in New Cross. It was widely suspected to have been a racially motivated arson attack by someone outside the property, and the police investigation was criticised as inadequate for not exploring that possibility.

Black activists, including Darcus Howe, organised a march for the "Black People's Day of Action" on 2 March. Up to 25,000 attended the march. The marchers walked 17 miles from Deptford to Hyde Park, passing the Houses of Parliament and Fleet Street. The national newspapers papers unloaded their full weight of racial stereotyping.

At the beginning of April 1981, the Metropolitan Police began *Operation Swamp 81*. Officers from other Metropolitan police districts and the Special Patrol Group were dispatched into Brixton, and within five days, 943 black people were stopped and searched, and 82 arrested, through the heavy use of what was colloquially known as the "Sus" law. This law allowed police to search and arrest members of the public when it was believed that they were acting suspiciously, and not necessarily committing a crime. The African-Caribbean community were disproportionately targeted by the police using these powers against black people.

Promise Owens Otikor

I had a friend named Promise. I always thought it was an incredible and improbable name, but it was his real name. He was Nigerian Igbo like me and about 7 years older than me. Initially when he came to London from Nigeria he lived in our house in Battersea that was set out over 3 floors. My parents had bought the house in the 1960s and rented out some of the rooms to help pay the mortgage.

Promise rented one of the rooms and became a close friend and a kind of mentor. We talked a lot about the spiritual world and we drank a lot of beer and smoked a lot of cigarettes together.

Our family lived in the basement flat that has 2 rooms. The rest of the rooms were all above over 3 floors with up to 4 different people renting rooms from my parents at any one time.

Promise always wore boots and a neat blazer. He was a permanent Accountancy student, studying Cost & Management Accountancy and doing night-time security work to pay for his studies. Had a 'tab' at the local grocery where he settled his bill weekly. Sometimes Promise would send me over to the grocery store for a loaf of bread or something similar, and I would tell the manager it was for Promise. The manager would write it down and say ok, and then I would take whatever it was without paying and take it to promise.

Once a guy named George who was always jealous of Promise went to the grocery store and saw me get something for Promise without paying. When I had gone, George asked the store manager how much money promise owed. The grocery store manager later on told Promise, who unsurprisingly, was furious that George was snooping into his private business. Promise said to George that he must be wanting to pay his bill if he is so concerned about his private accounts, and he made George go and pay his bill for him.

By the time I was 18 years old Promise had left our house and was living in his own flat that was on the same street directly opposite our house. I used to pop across the road and visit him regularly. He held a lot of wild parties with lots of weed, alcohol and women.

At the age of 18 years old, a few days before I was scheduled to go to Nigeria, I went to visit Promise. Because we were both of Nigerian heritage there was an acknowledgement between us that my trip to Nigeria was important for my knowledge of myself and where my parents came from. But we both felt that something wasn't quite right about my trip. I remember looking out of the window of his lounge to my house across the street, and wondering why did I feel that I might never be coming back from Nigeria.

LESSONS LEARNED FROM MY MOTHER AND FATHER

My mother and father were passionate about education. I learned from them that education holds the key to whatever you want to achieve.

I also learned that there is no excuse to stop you from going forward in life. My parents left their home country to make a new life for themselves and go forward in life.

My mother was a devout Christian, but ironically it was me who taught her that 'God helps those who help themselves'.

MY FOSTER FAMILY

My white working-class family

In the 1960's and 1970s, thousands of Nigerian families fostered their children to mainly white working class British parents. The process was called "Farming", because the children were farmed out. The idea was that the children would integrate better and more easily into British society. My parents were students at the time I was fostered.

It was for me, mainly a good experience, and I got on well with my foster family, who already had 4 children of their own before they fostered me. Unfortunately, many Nigerian children who were fostered, developed serious identity crises and self-loathing. Some were even suicidal about the conflict with their British identity and their African heritage.

Not all Nigerian children suffered a sense of self alienation, but many Nigerian children went through a particular kind of mental psychosis that is brought about by a temporary or total rejection of their colour and cultural heritage.

From the age of about 6 months, or maybe a year old until I was aged between 6 years old and 11 years old, I lived with a white working class family. Then I went back to live with my Nigerian parents. It was a difficult transition from my white family back to my Nigerian parents. Even though they visited me weekly, I had no memory of them at all. Apparently, my real parents visited me regularly, but I had no knowledge or memory of them until I was about 6 or 7 years old. My Nigerian siblings, Abi, Ifeoma and Chiatulah lived with my biological Nigerian parents.

I was the only one of 6 siblings in my family to be fostered, although my mother once told me that my brother Chiat was fostered for about 1 year.

From the age of about 7 years old, I used to run away from my Nigerian parents back to my foster parents. I'd stay with my foster parents for a week or so, and one of my foster sisters would bring me back to my biological parents, with me and my foster sister Theresa both crying. That carried on and off for about a year.

At one point there were two entrances to my Nigerian parents' house. One entrance was on street level, and the other entrance at the front of the house, up some stairs. You could go from the bottom of the house and come out through the front upstairs and vice versa. I used this technique to initially outwit my Dad and run away back to my foster parents. But my Dad started to catch me. I eventually gave up running away and submitted to my fate to live with my Nigerian parents who I didn't know or understand.

Foster family

I had a very happy life with my foster parents. I went from sleeping on a normal bed with my foster family, to sleeping on a camp bed in the lounge with my Nigerian family. This was a huge shock and surprise to me, and even at that young age

I thought why are they having me here when they don't have any space for me?

Toilet with my real parents was outside, filled with cobwebs and spiders. It was a real challenge and experience staying focussed when doing a number 2.

When I wasn't happy at my Nigerian parents' house, I just ran away and I stayed with my foster family for a week or two. Then my foster sister Theresa would bring me back to my biological parents. Along the way on the walk back to my real parents, I would be crying, and Theresa would be crying too. That happened many times. One of my favourite songs at the time was by Steve Harley & Cockney Rebel called, 'Come Up And See Me– Make Me Smile'. The song made me sad because I used to wish that my foster sister Theresa would come to visit me at my Nigerian parents' house, and take me back with her to stay with them.

My foster parents lived close to my biological parents it was a 10 minute walk.

They took me to Cornwall with them and their children during the school holidays for up to 6 weeks at a time. I remember once we stopped at a cinema along the way on the journey from London to Cornwall. We watched the film 'Bedknobs and Broomsticks', which became a favourite of mine for years after. The magic of the fantasy really knocked me out.

My foster mother took me to West Ham United football matches. My foster family were all West Ham fanatics, and every birthday as a child my foster mum used to buy me some form of West Ham United memorabilia. It was most often a sports bag, but occasionally a West Ham shirt or kit. The only West ham matches we went to were when West Ham played Chelsea. The reason was that Chelsea football ground wasn't too far from where we lived in Wandsworth.

When I was six or seven not all my siblings were born. There was Chiatulah, one year after me, Ifeoma was four years younger than me. Chiatulah would have been six. Ifeoma would have been two or three. And Abi is two years younger than Ifeoma. Nnabuike and Chiduve wouldn't have been born yet.

By the time I was aged 11, all of my siblings had been born and I was living with all of my siblings with my Nigerian parents. I was then the oldest of 6. I was the youngest of five when I lived with my foster family.

When I lived with my foster parents they had a cellar which was full of large sacks of coal. I used to sometimes help get coal from their cellar, and I was always surprised how deep it was. From the outside of the house you would never imagine it was so huge. It was like a small underground house in itself.

Like most children I had no interest in politics. But one thing stayed with me that I could never understand. In the late 1960's the British Conservative Government Education Secretary was Margaret Thatcher. She ended free school milk for children aged over 7 years. In those days we used to get free milk and sometimes free orange juice. Both came in small glass bottles. It was one of the highlights of the school day and teachers used the promise of getting our milk as a way to help improve our behaviour. Or punish us by not allowing us milk if we'd misbehaved.

I'll never forget the day when our teacher announced that there would be no more free milk as the government had decided to take it away from the children. For many years after, I could never understand why anyone would be so cruel to children.

In the media she became known as 'Thatcher – The Milk Snatcher!'

I went to a Roman Catholic secondary school in Clapham. It was a good school and an all -boys school. The tradition at the school was that if a parent of one of the students died, there would be a Mass said in the school in the school church. I remember that when one of my peers father died, the school church was packed. But when my father died hardly anyone attended the school service. That broke my heart. I wouldn't say that the fact that I was black and my peers father was white had anything to do with it. But I always wondered about that. What it did do was put me in my place, and give me a painful wake up call. I wasn't as popular as I thought I was.

When I was 12 years old, an Outreach Youth worker by the name of Mick Owens went around the streets asking young people to get involved in a committee to set up a youth club. I became a committee member of the youth council that led to the setting up of a youth club for our area. I attended and remained a member of that youth club up until I was about 16 years old.

Chased by skinheads

Britain's first black feature film,' Pressure' is the story of the plight of disenchanted British-born black youths. Set in 1970s South London, not far from where I grew up, it tells the story of Tony, a bright school-leaver, son of West Indian immigrants, who finds himself torn between his parents' church-going conformity and his brother's Black Power militancy.

As his initially high hopes are repeatedly dashed – he cannot find work anywhere, potential employers treat him with suspicion because of his colour – his sense of alienation grows. In a bid to find a sense of belonging, he joins his black friends who, estranged from their submissive parents, seek a sense of purpose in the streets and in chases with the police.

The film fully encapsulated and expressed my anger, and the identity struggles that children of immigrants had to face.

In the 1980 film 'Babylon' the lead character is a south London garage-hand by day and a disco-dispenser by night. The film follows the young black male Dancehall DJ as he loses his job as a car mechanic, struggles with his racist boss, gets beaten up by police, is falsely charged, and forced to go on the run, falling out with his girlfriend and finally stabbing a racist neighbour in anger and frustration. The film finishes with a posse of policemen smashing down the doors of a music hall.

The racist political group The National Front comprised of large numbers of 'skinheads' were on the rise in 1970s London. The film shows his battles against those forces and reflected mine and many other young black men's experience of growing up in London in the 1970s.

One afternoon in the summer of 1980 when I was 16 years old, me and Michael Kavanagh a white guy, were in central London near Trafalgar square just hanging out. A large group of racist skinheads who were in the National Front were on a march. They saw me and Mikey and called him names for hanging out with a "nigger". Then suddenly they were chasing after us! At first me and Mikey ran together in the same direction, but without saying a word to each other we split up and ran in different directions. I managed to get away, but they caught Mikey and beat him up.

Part-time job in Tesco

Me and Mikey had been friends from a very early age in primary school, and we went to the same secondary school. He was part of my 'Dragon-Ace-Face-Karavan Club' when we were 8 or 9 years old. That name was formed from the nicknames of the four club members. My nickname was 'Dragon' inspired by the dragon motif on the forearms of the character 'Kwai Chang Caine' who was a master of martial arts and a priest from the Chinese Shaolin Temple, in the American action drama series called 'Kung Fu'. At age 16 me and Mikey were working together in part-time jobs in Tesco. I always used to dress really sharp in silk shirts and bright red or yellow or white ties. Every saturday after I got paid I'd go straight to a clothes shop and buy a new shirt and tie. The Tesco manager, Mr Arnold, used to compliment me on how well I dressed.

Me, Mikey and a mixed group of black and white part-time workers used to treat the Tesco warehouse as our personal canteen. We'd deliberately drop a box of biscuits which would damage one or two packets inside. This meant that the whole box had to be discarded. It also meant free food for whoever wanted it. The only problem was we weren't allowed to do it. But almost everyone did at some point.

Some of us set up a scam where we put goods outside the back of the shop next to a 'baling machine' that was meant for destroying boxes.

At the end of the evening, on our way home after the store had closed, some of us would go to the back of the store and collect our stolen goods that were disguised as rubbish.

It became a huge operation. So many staff got involved. It was like a mini-corporation, with people ordering goods that they wanted. One evening after work I went to the back of the store by the baling machine to collect a box of chocolates I'd stashed there. To my dismay, there was a long queue of people who were waiting to collect stolen goods. Many of the people were members of the general public who didn't work in the store.

The whole thing had become too open and exposed. Right there and then I decided to quit stealing from the store. Surely it would be just a matter of a few days before the management became aware of what was going on.

I ended up getting sacked due to being caught for eating just one biscuit from a genuinely broken packet in the warehouse.

The manager Mr Arnold was the one who caught me. He took me up to his office and told me that he was sorry that he would have to let me go. He said it was a real pity because I was a nice guy, and the best dressed worker he's ever had.

The human chain

I knew a group of teenagers who lived around my area who were into crime. They weren't professionals, but were always on the lookout for an opportunity to make money. Legally or illegally. Across the road from where I lived was a main high street lined with every kind of shop. The shops backed on to a row of houses. One of the crew I knew discovered that you could go around to the back of the shops, climb a wall and get to the back doors of the shops.

He broke into one of the shops and called up some of his friends and began stealing food and drinks from the grocery shop. Word spread very quickly and a human chain was set up leading from the street to the back of the shop. Goods were passed along the chain to the safe part of the street and shared out afterwards. One night I was invited to join the chain by the crew leader. An assistant of his didn't want me to be involved because I looked too soft. Foolishly I asserted myself and claimed that I wasn't as soft as he thought and I joined the 'human shop stealing chain'. I wanted to be a part of the crew and hoped to gain their respect and friendship and even their protection, if I ever needed it. I went on a few raids with them until one evening someone saw us all and called the police. In minutes police sirens were blaring and most of us got away, but some were caught by the police. I got away.

I thought of what my dead father and my mother and my foster parents would have thought. I didn't want my brothers and sisters to think less of me as their older brother. I also was very clear that if I carried on this way I was certain to go to prison and ruin my life in the process. I wanted more for myself than that. I made a promise to myself to stop immediately and never get involved with those guys again. I was at a crossroads in my life. I chose to be positive and turn my life from negative to positive.

Role models

I used to watch a weekly music show called 'Top of The Pops'. It show-cased the most diverse range of music from all over the UK and from other countries too. In the late 70s Bob Marley's reggae music began to have a huge impact on the white British pop music scene. I bought a '7 inch' reggae record called 'Dreadlock Holiday' by the white British pop group '10cc'. It was the first record I ever bought, even though I didn't have a record player.

One of my foster sisters, Theresa, was an obsessed David Bowie fan. She was also an amazing artist and used to do a lot of paintings. She did her own painted version of David Bowie's Diamond Dogs LP cover. She made me into a semi Bowie fan.

There were almost no black male role models in the media for young black boys when I was growing up in London. So we looked to America. I became aware of Casius Clay because he was talked about a lot in the UK.

Before the world's greatest boxer Mohammed Ali became Mohammed Ali, he was Casius Clay. Shortly after Cassius Clay knocked-out Sonny Liston to earn his first world heavyweight championship title, he announced he was converting to Islam and becoming a member of Nation of Islam. A few weeks after his victory he adopted the Muslim name Muhammad Ali.

Before landing on the name Muhammad Ali, he briefly went by the name Cassius X, a nod to his friend and spiritual mentor Malcolm X, who had drawn him toward the inner circle of the Nation of Islam. Ali became a political figure in 1967 for refusing to be drafted into the armed forces during the Vietnam War. He was so popular that my foster mother and even other white people loved him.

My foster mother also loved "The Harlem Globe Trotters", widely acknowledged as the best all African-American basketball team in history. 'Harlem Globetrotters', was a Hanna-Barbera saturday morning cartoon, broadcast from September 12, 1970, to May 1973. Originally broadcast on CBS and later rerun on NBC as The Go-Go Globetrotters.

The series worked to a formula where the all African-American team travels somewhere and typically get involved in a local conflict that leads to one of the Globetrotters proposing a basketball game to settle the issue. To ensure the Globetrotters' defeat, the villains rig the contest; however, before the second half of the contest, the team always finds a way to even the odds, become all but invincible, and win the game.

The Harlem Globetrotters were like spiritual warriors to me. They were heroes who I could identify with who weren't misrepresented as criminals. Being a sports star was an accepted profession for a young black male. But I was more into the arts as a potential future career.

LESSONS LEARNED FROM MY FOSTER FAMILY

My foster mother taught me to read properly when I was struggling at the age of around four or five years old.

I learned the value of compassion, maturity and affection from my foster mother and father, and from my foster brothers and sisters.

JOYCE

I met Joyce when I was 16 years old. We were both the same age, and I was just a few months older. Her parents were from Guyana, and she had 2 younger sisters and an older brother. We met at a party in a house of mutual friends where I asked her for a dance, and it took us only one dance before we both fell in love straight away. When it was time to go home, we exchanged phone numbers and I called her the very next day. We talked for hours on the phone about our hopes, dreams and ambitions. We knew we were in love and we celebrated that by writing each other very long love letters on a regular basis.

When I first went to visit her, at the age of 16, it was the furthest I'd ever travelled to on my own in London. Joyce lived in Edmonton, which was about a two -hour journey by bus and tube, and I'd never been to Edmonton. I was quite nervous about travelling so far from home on my own, so I spoke to my foster mother about my plan to visit Joyce and asked her the best way to get there. Somehow, I managed to pretend to myself that I was brave and kept my fears inside for the sake of love. When I finally arrived at her house I was nervous and excited at the same time. Joyce saw me arrive and opened the door, as she'd been looking out of her downstairs lounge windows, waiting near the door to make sure she could see me coming.

Dating the old-fashioned way

She showed me into the lounge, invited me to sit down and said she will be back shortly. I got the biggest shock of my life a few minutes later when the door opened, and instead of Joyce was her father!! He had come down to have a talk with me about what were my intentions with his daughter!

After he'd finished making me feel small and unworthy, he left the room. I almost considered calling the whole thing off with Joyce, then her sisters who had been upstairs, came down and asked me if I'm alright. I said that I was fine, and pretended that it was no stress at all. But inside I was still shocked and shaken. Joyce came down soon afterwards, and she saw that really, I was disturbed and uncomfortable. Her concern and caring convinced me that for me to be with her, it was worth all the stress and hassle with her father.

Once Joyce bought a multi- coloured jumper for me. Exactly the same as one that she'd bought for herself. A lot of my peers wouldn't have been seen dead wearing the same jumper as their girlfriend, but I loved it and was proud to wear it with her. When we went out we often made sure our clothes matched each other.

In those days in the soul music scene DJ's used to hold events called "all-dayers". Me and Joyce took the train to an 'all-dayer' at a seaside town and danced with hundreds of others to the great soul tune hits of that time such as "Searching" by a group called 'Change' featuring the singer Luther Vandross. Another favourite was "Jingo" by the group ' Candido'. On the way back home, on the train, I fell asleep cuddled up next to Joyce. She later told me that she'd been physically intimate with me while I was asleep. I laughed and was surprised because up until then she'd been very conservative.

We used to go regularly to 'All Nations' night club in East London. It was open from 10pm until 6am the next morning every Friday and Saturday, and we always stayed all night, dancing almost non-stop for the whole night in each other's arms. It had three floors of music. One floor soul, one floor reggae and one floor mixed soul, reggae and Soca music. One of our favourite reggae 'lovers rock' songs was "Paradise" by Jean Adebambo. I never liked Soca music, but most people at that time went crazy about it.

Almost every week from the age of 16 to 18 years old, we wrote long love letters, with poems and songs to each other. Even at that young age we fantasized about getting married and wanted to be together for ever. All our friends thought that we'd get married too.

LESSONS LEARNED FROM MY LIFE WITH JOYCE

I learned what real love is from Joyce.

I learned what being in a relationship can only really work best when two people share the same interests, have the same attitude to life, and most importantly, are best friends.

SPRINGFIELD Mental Health Hospital (AKA Looney Bin)

The Devils Bum Club!

At the age of 18 I was studying 'A' Level Art with a small group of students in the 6th form in school. The dream for most, if not all of us was to be film directors. We discussed the latest films all the time and action thrillers were our favourites.

We used to play around in the art room at lunchtime and it became like a club room for us. We decided to give our group a name and wanted to come up with the most outrageous name we could think of, just for fun. We decided to call ourselves 'The Devils Bum Club!' They were Ian, Chris, Sean, Lobo, Karl d'M and Kevin O. Sometimes we would drag one of the younger students of the school into the Art room at lunchtime and tease them that if they didn't do their homework or if they misbehaved, The Devils Bum would get them! We laughed hysterically over that.

We were heavily influenced by and inspired by Bruce Lee's "Enter The Dragon". We knew almost all of the words in the film and had endless discussions about the film. Inspired by Bruce Lee films, I enrolled in a karate club for a while, in a small church very close to Battersea Park. The teachers name was Jeff Whybrow. He was charismatic and inspired respect.

In the art room at lunchtime we used to mess around and practice martial arts kicks on the art easels. One day Miss Mooney, our art teacher, came in at lunchtime and saw me do a karate kick and smash two of the easels, leaving it in pieces on the floor. She wasn't angry or upset, she just said that I need to be more careful in future! She had a great sense of perspective. She knew we were good kids who worked very hard in our 'A' levels and we were just blowing off steam. I didn't last long at the karate club as I didn't have the self-discipline to train and practice.

In 1979 a space horror film came out called "Alien". The monster was designed by an artist called HR Giger. Hans Ruedi Giger was a Swiss painter, best known for airbrush images of humans and machines linked together in a cold biomechanical relationship. He was part of the special effects team that won an Academy Award for design work on the film "Alien". The film was another big influence on the art education of "The Devils Bum Club". As a result, we all got really into airbrush art and all bought books to study Gigers art.

How did I end up in Springfield?

I'd been smoking too much weed while doing 'A' level Art. In addition I wasn't eating enough, due to being lost in the trance-like state of concentrating while painting. One day at lunchtime in school in the art room, I decided to home to get some money for food as I'd forgotten to bring in lunch money. Because I didn't have any money on me I had to walk home. On my way home, I started hallucinating through a mixture of hunger and tiredness, made worse by having smoked too much weed.

The next thing I knew was that it was night time and my mother and a group of people were crying and praying around me, in the lounge in our house. I ran to the church and the church door was open. I went into pray. The next thing I knew was being bundled into an ambulance and taken to hospital in the middle of the night, by a group consisting of local priest, family and friends of my mother.

Springfield Hospital

The first ward I was in was a lock-down ward. Like a prison. I went through about three or four rooms accompanied by two big guards who locked each door behind us as we passed though. Finally, we reached a large room about 20 metres square with only three or four chairs in it and one or 2 small tables.

Leading off from the room was a small staircase that led upstairs to our sleeping area. It had about 5 or six beds, but only two or three other people slept there when I slept there. I had nightmares of death and dying every night in that upstairs sleeping room. I also often dreamt about and God and my dead father and seeing demons.

I spent my days just walking around the room. The beds were upstairs close to the big room. Visitors could come to the big room and see you.

I had to take six or seven large pills several times a day with water. Taking the medication my brain slowed down and I could hardly think or even talk properly. It also made walking very difficult. I knew I had to stop taking the medication as I felt that the longer I took the medication, the longer it would take me to get better.

And I seriously felt that to keep taking the medication would make me permanently mentally ill. I thought to myself, I may never get out of there.

Padded Cell

One day I decided to stop taking the medication. Two or three big burly guys in white coats came and tried to force me to take the medication. I fought like a wounded lion, as best as I could, but they got the better of me. Then they gave me an injection and put me in a straight-jacket, and put me in a padded cell, and locked the door. The room was tiny about 10ft by 10 feet. It had no widows except for a small window in the door to give me food. The walls were all white, and all I could do was lay on the floor. Sometimes I screamed and rolled around on the floor writhing and trying to get out of the straight jacket. But I was no Harry Houdini.

Open ward

I was kept in the padded cell for about 3 days and nights and slept on the floor as there was no bed. They let me out into an open ward after they felt I was calm enough to keep taking the medication. There were about five or six other people on the ward with me. It was a mixed gender ward with male and female together. One white male and the rest of African and Caribbean heritage. At age 17, I was the youngest, the rest were all appeared to be in their 30s or 40. I could move around freely and there was no strict regime apart from breakfast and lunch.

I really missed not having my music around me and was really bored most of the time. At bedtime, I hated going to bed and felt as though I was a prisoner. But I noticed that no-one really checked up on you in the open ward.

I read science journals, and discussed the latest scientific developments with another guy who was also in there of African-Caribbean heritage.

Escape from Springfield

One day, I decided to leave the hospital premises. I really wanted my music, so I calmly got dressed and luckily found some money in one of my pockets. I was going to go home and get my music. I really thought that it was quite a silly idea, and that as soon as I left the ward someone was likely to ask me where was I going. I really didn't think I would get far, but then I thought, what the hell, I've nothing to lose.

I walked out of the ward and along a long driveway and fully expected someone to stop me. I was surprised that it was really quiet and no one seemed to be around.

As I began to get closer to the exit gate I started to panic, because I thought that knowing my luck, I'll get very close to the gate then I'll be stopped. To my surprise and shock I got to the gate and no one had stopped me! I couldn't believe it! I walked through the gate looking around me wondering where all the security was. No one tried to stop me. As I ventured out into the street to look for a bus, it crossed my mind that I could go home and not come back. Who was to know? I went home.

When I arrived home, I was hoping that I could get in and out quickly and that no-one at home would see me. I didn't want to have to try and explain why I was out, and it was embarrassing enough that I was in the mental hospital in the first place.

Being certified as mentally ill wasn't something I ever imagined or expected would happen to me. At home, I briefly saw my mum and sister who were both very surprised to see me. I went up to my bedroom, got my radio cassette player, then went back to Springfield. All along the journey I was drugged up and wasn't sure if I would make it back to the hospital without passing out. What surprised me is that when I got back to Springfield, nobody noticed that I was gone!

About two years before I was dragged off to Springfield, I went there with a friend to visit my friend's mum. I said to myself, I will never end up in here.

Visitors to Springfield

When Joyce and her mum came to visit me, I thought I was hallucinating or maybe just dreaming. The drugs had made me very confused and slowed down my thinking capability. It wasn't a dream, Joyce was real. But I wished that her mum wasn't real! I felt ashamed and embarrassed. But happy to see Joyce when I finally realised that she was real. The fact that Joyce came to visit me meant so much to me. I loved her so much for that visit. I played my favourite song at that time to her, it was "Let's Celebrate" by the group 'Skyy'. I loved the lyric, ' you might think I'm going insane, hey baby let's break out the champagne '.

My brother Chiat came to see me several times. We joked and laughed and I told him how they put me in a straight-jacket and locked me up. Despite my trying to lighten the mood, we both understood the seriousness of the situation.

Probably the biggest shock of all for me was being visited in Springfield by my 'A' Level Art teacher, Miss Mooney. Me and the Devil's Bum Club crew had been in love with her, ever since she first began teaching us several years earlier. She looked so sad when she came to see me, but also had so much compassion and care in her eyes. I was really humbled and honoured that she came to see me. She didn't have to. It showed to me how much she cared about me as one of her students.

After Springfield

I was in Springfield Mental Hospital for about three weeks. Leaving Springfield was a relief and a surprise to me. I thought that I'd be trapped in there for quite a few months. I had a review with a psychiatrist who cleared me and remarked at how amazed he was at my quick recovery. He set up some appointments for me to see him after I'd left Springfield and review my progress.

I saw him twice afterwards at Bolingbroke Hospital. The same hospital that I used to go and visit my dad before he died. I was originally scheduled to see the psychiatrist for a minimum of six sessions, but after the second session he told me that I didn't need to see him anymore.

I needed to finish my education, so I went back to school at Clapham College Secondary School. I was quite worried about what teachers and students would say about my three -week disappearance.

I was given a warm and friendly welcome, and interrogated in a good humoured and low-key way by "The Devils' Bum

Club!". For the rest of the school it was as though nothing had happened.

One of the art teachers, a woman named Cheryl Drower, accidentally told me that Miss Mooney my art teacher, had some of my paintings I had done in her Art class. She had put my paintings on the wall at her home in her dining room!

Soon after I'd come out of Springfield, Joyce held a party at her house to celebrate my return. I wore a multi-coloured jumper my foster mum knitted for me. It was the same jumper I had taken in with me to Springfield. Forever afterwards that jumper signified freedom for me. For a little while at the party, I danced alone in the front room in Joyce's house late at night after everyone had gone home. I stayed overnight at Joyce's house and we slept together on the sofa in the lounge.

Joyce used to always bring down a blanket from her bedroom, and we used to cuddle up together under the blanket on the sofa. Her sisters used to politely stay in their bedroom when I used to visit.

LESSONS LEARNED FROM MY TIME IN SPRINGFIELD

I learned that the influence of a committed teacher or mentor can really help to inspire and change a person's life from negative to positive.

Positive influences of teachers, youth workers and mentors in my life provided the same inspiration for me to become a youth worker, teaching assistant and learning mentor, to try and help and inspire others too.

NIGERIA

London 1982

I will never forget summer 1982. It was a glorious time for me. I was probably the happiest I had been in my whole life. Britain had recently won the Falklands War, but I didn't care about that. I was 18 years old and legally independent. I was actually independent long before then, but now I was officially my own person. I had a part time job, and I was getting a study grant. The first thing I did with my grant money (which was about 200 pounds per term) was to go out and buy myself a radio-cassette player. It became my best friend and I took it with me everywhere.

I had my life planned out and I was doing 'A' levels in Art and English in the 6th Form at Clapham College Secondary school which had transitioned from a grammar school to a comprehensive school. I didn't have my results yet. They would come out in August and I was looking forward to getting them, and ready to enjoy the summer holidays.

The day after I broke up from school my mum said to me, "Would you like to go on a holiday to Nigeria?". I said "No I'm not interested". Neither me or any of my siblings wanted to go, but she managed to persuade us. She said it's just for a two- week holiday. I was the eldest of 6 siblings. Three brothers and two sisters. When my father died when I was 13, I became my own person. If there was anything my mother wanted me to do and I didn't want to do it, there was nothing she could tell me. It would stop there. But, I decided to always do my best to help my mother.

My brother Chiatulah was a year younger than me. Before we left for Nigeria, my mum gave me and Chiat some money to buy clothes and told us to buy suits. She wanted us to impress the people we would see in Nigeria. So, I went out and bought three suits. A pale blue one, a white one, and a cream one. I went to the West End of London and I bought suits I really liked. Really flashy ones. Me, my mum and 3 of my other younger siblings packed just enough clothes for two weeks.

I was a good son, but I had lived a very hedonistic teenage life. I regularly sneaked out at night to go to late night reggae parties in old abandoned houses. Somehow managing to get up for school the next mornings. I worked part time, and from the age of 14 I had a paper round. By the time I was 16 that was it. I was my own man.

I had a girlfriend Joyce at the time, who I was deeply in love with. We were in a very serious relationship and were both aged 16 when we met. We became one almost immediately on first sight of each other. She lived in Edmonton which was almost a two-hour journey from where I lived. I met her at a party in Battersea when she came to visit a friend of her cousin who lived close to me. We fell in love at virtually first dance, and exchanged address and phone numbers. We wrote long letters to each other and we developed a deep emotional bond. Not like texts today. I would send her 5-page love letters and she'd reply back with six-page love letters. The James Bond film The Spy Who Loved Me was shown on ITV. I loved the films theme song "Nobody Does It Better" by Carly Simon. It made me think of her.

The night before I was due to go to Nigeria, me and Joyce were at a party, both of us were aged 18 at this time. I went outside to stand and have a cigarette. It was the middle of the night, maybe 2am and she came out with me. She said, "Ed, I have a bad feeling about Nigeria. Don't go". She begged me not to go. I said," Don't be silly, I'm only going for two weeks, I'll be back soon". But that was a lie. I had a bad feeling about it too. Something didn't feel right. I tried to be the macho man and pretend that I wasn't afraid, so that she wouldn't be afraid, and to show her that I was a strong man.

Arrival in Lagos

In Nigeria the first place we arrived was Lagos. When we got off the plane it was as though I'd put my head in an oven. I wondered how could I survive the heat for one day, let alone two weeks. Then once we were at the airport we couldn't get out!

At the customs and immigration barrier we were there for about two hours, but not due to normal checks. There was no way they would let us through until we had settled the bribe. I was worried that we would be stuck in the airport, humiliated and stranded.

By the time we finally got out of the airport, me and my siblings were anxious, nervous and very worried. Now I was really certain that it had been a big mistake to come to Nigeria.

My mother was trying to find us a taxi, when about three or four guys ran up to us and snatched our bags pulling all of us in different directions. We fought back screaming for them to get away. I didn't know they were taxi drivers. They had no identification and looked as though they were angry and wanted to fight us.

My mum told me that what they were doing was the normal way to get your custom. I couldn't believe it. That was normal practice! It was the only way for them to get customers because the competition was so brutally fierce. It was a horrific introduction into Nigeria. I thought that things must surely get better from here on. Perhaps this was the worst of it and things would be calmer like a normal holiday. I felt very uneasy and became more and more worried in my mind as my mother didn't seem to be well organised. My siblings were all shocked and scared too.

Eventually we made it into a taxi and we went to stay with a family friend in Lagos who was seemingly well off. We thought this is not too bad. Nice place, nice part of Lagos. We stayed overnight and for one day. But it was a false dawn. I mentally prepared myself for our next destination which was to be Onitsha. I knew it was going to be a challenge because we knew that the relatives we were going to stay with in Onitsha were very poor. Onitsha was a market town. At one point in time it was the largest market in the whole of West Africa. The houses there were a mixture of low rise blocks and falling apart sheds.

We got on the coach down to Onitsha and hell began again. Everyday a new hell began. It was a long, miserable and cramped journey, took about 18 hours, and was hot all the way with no air conditioning inside. The coaches were beaten, bashed, broken, dusty and dirty. People sat on each other's laps and luggage was packed in the aisles so you couldn't move. A lot of the luggage was loosely tied to the roof and I'm sure that I heard some of it fall off from the roof along the way.

The driver acted as though he was on a cocktail of alcohol, cocaine and a whole range of other drugs all combined. I didn't think we had long to live with him driving. Even the good roads were treacherous, and the bad roads were just suicidal. He drove like a mad man, challenging death to try and catch us. There were no traffic lights or road markings, so people drove without any care for lanes or overtaking. We stopped only twice in 18 hours for everyone to relieve themselves in the bush, and we were told to watch out for snakes! There were never toilets anywhere.

Onitsha Market Town - Betrayal

When we arrived in Onitsha, this is it, I thought to myself, we've entered the deepest depths of Hell. The sandy streets were all deep red, it was somehow even hotter than Lagos and deafeningly noisy. Every second shop was a music shop or people just played music whatever shop it was. A cacophony of blaring, screaming, screeching sounds, all trying to compete with each other to see who could play their music the loudest. You couldn't hear yourself think.

There was no law or rules. So you could blast your music at the highest volume. And everybody did. I was sure that I wouldn't be able to cope. I thought I would die in a few minutes, from the sound and the heat. That was my introduction to Onitsha. For me, it was a nightmare. And it got worse.

We met with my aunt 'Ma'Peter'. Her name was a colloquial abbreviation of "Mother of Peter", and she was the sister of my dead father. She was delighted to see us but I had an uneasy feeling about her. We saw my brother Chiduve and my brother Nnabuike. They were my two youngest siblings. It was a heart-breaking and tearful reunion. They had been in Nigeria since my mother had taken my fathers' body and buried him there 7 years before we arrived. She'd taken them with her for the burial, and left them in Nigeria all that time. I felt so sad to see them living under the conditions that they were living. It broke my heart. Chiduve would have been 7 years old and Nnabuike would have been around 9 years old.

We had come from London, and they all thought we lived in the lap of luxury. They were barefoot, and Chiduve was in raggedy torn shorts, barefoot, and in a worn out, dirty old t-shirt selling water on the street. I thought to myself, this is my brother this is the life he lives. I was barely able to contain my tears. He had the worst experience of the 6 of us. His story may never be told. I was crushed that my own brothers couldn't speak English to me at that time, maybe only a few words. It tore me apart.

My mum was struggling with the situation and heart-broken too. 'Ma'Peter' hated Chiduve and loved Nnabuike and she expressed that fully in the way she treated them differently. Chiduve was out on the streets barefoot selling water. Nnabuike was bought clothes and sent to school. Chiduve wasn't allowed to go to school. She used to beat him all the time. Nnabuike was treated like a king.

Ajassa Street, was one of the main streets leading to the market of Onitsha. About midway one of the many record shops played a song called “Hypertension”. The song was played non- stop daily by one of the music shop owners, I was sure that it was part of a plan to drive me mad. Or maybe it was all just a horrible nightmare? My relationship with my relatives in Nigeria was strange and very uncomfortable. I had never met them before and knew absolutely nothing at all about them.

It was a very painful, sad and difficult relationship, because I was so sad and unhappy about the way my brothers had been treated. Inside myself I was crying and dying, and I was constantly thinking of how we could get them away from all this and bring them back to London with us. This wasn’t what I hoped for or expected to see. This was no holiday. It was a disaster, and I just wanted it to be over as soon as possible to get back to London.

I’d been in Nigeria for about about 4 or 5 days. So far, my whole experience had been one of disappointment and sadness. I’d worked hard to keep up my spirits and not show how upset I was. I was still looking forward to getting back to London. It was morning and I was sitting on the steps outside the room I shared with my brother Chiat in Onitsha. The room was just 10 or 15 metres from Ma’Peters food shack. I had nothing to do and was just idling away time. My sisters were with my mother and my brother Chiat was over in the nearby shack having something to eat. “Ma’Peter’s” son Peter came up to me and said, “Let’s go for a walk”. Initially I thought fine, maybe we’ll go somewhere interesting maybe he will say that it was a bad idea that we visited Nigeria and it was a big mistake for me and my siblings to come and visit them when they were all in such a bad situation and struggling financially. We walked slowly along the road together, which was tricky and dangerous as there was no pavement, and Peter said to me, "How would you feel about staying here in Nigeria?"

At first, I didn't understand the question. I thought he was perhaps trying to find out how I felt about my cultural heritage after me having been born in London and grown up in London. Part of me thought this was a ridiculous question. I had an Arts School place set up to study for a degree in Graphic Design. I said to him, "Well there are things I have to do in London. And I have a girlfriend who is waiting for me. We have plans". Then he said to me, "You are staying. Whether you like it or not! Your passports have been taken and there's nothing you can do about it!"

Millions of thoughts went through my mind.

Something about the way he said it, made me know intuitively in my gut that there was nothing I could do about it. It was clear to me that he knew something that I didn't know.

I felt sick to my stomach. I vomited and Peter didn't care. I couldn't breathe. I thought I was going to have a heart attack right there and then. I was bewildered and in total shock and disbelief. It was beyond surreal. I wanted to vomit, I wanted to cry out in anguish. I felt as though I was trapped inside my body and couldn't get out of my body. It was worse than being in prison. You can try and escape from prison, but it's not so easy to escape from a country. Especially when you have no passport and no money and no means of getting either. Where did this insane idea come from?

I felt so completely destroyed and betrayed. Why did my Mum allow this? How could she do this to me? What did I do to deserve this? Was I such a bad kid? Why wasn't I allowed to decide my own future? I was 18, old enough to get married without anyone's permission, for God's sake!! My soul felt crushed. I quickly lost heart and I lost all hope of ever being free.

It was too shocking and unbelievable for me to comprehend, it was as though I had died and my spirit left my body, and I was outside of my body looking down at what was going on, and watching Peter telling me that I'm staying. I couldn't cry out although I wanted to. I couldn't scream and shout although I wanted to. I knew that I was doomed and trapped with absolutely no way out, because they had my passport and I didn't know where they had hidden it! It was the worst thing that had ever happened in my life and I couldn't believe or understand the injustice of it.

It was so stupid and ridiculous. I wanted to fight Peter and do him some serious harm. But I also knew that would just make things worse, and not solve the problem of how I could leave the country. I was furious and at the same time confused. How the hell had I ended up in this situation where I was a prisoner trapped in Nigeria against my will. Surely this was illegal kidnapping? But then who could I tell? Who could I turn to? There was no one, because I didn't know anyone else in Nigeria and I had no clue as to how things work in Nigeria. And because the person who had planned it all was my mother, there was absolutely no one I could turn to.

I felt it must have been a deliberate plan organised in partnership with 'MaPeter', my mother, and her relatives in Nigeria. That's the only way it could have worked. What was I to do? How did my relatives expect me to live? What kind of life did they think I would live in Nigeria with them, when they had no resources for our survival? It became clear to me almost immediately that there was absolutely no plan for what I was expected to do in Nigeria. No plans for a job, no plans for further education and no plan for where me and my siblings would live. We were on our own and had to find a way to survive by any means necessary.

My relatives and my mother completely disregarded my free will, and my plans and aims in London. I was 18 years old, and old enough to make my own decisions, and I had already made plans to go to art school in London after my "A" levels. My relatives and my mother didn't ask me about that. And they didn't care. The full freedom of my life that I'd had from 14 years old to 18 years old made it intolerably worse for my freedom to be taken away from me in such an unjustified manner.

I thought of Joyce and what she would think and how she somehow knew that I should not have gone to Nigeria. I wrote her a letter soon after I found out that I was being forced to stay. I foolishly and desperately hoped that she might organise a campaign to the government to get me out. It was devastating for me to have to admit to her that she was right about all the fears she had about me going to Nigeria and never returning back to London. I had tears in my eyes and tears in my heart when I wrote the letter to her about how I'd been forced to stay, and how unhappy I was, and that I had no idea when I would return to London, or if I would ever return.

I wondered if she would believe me, or think I'm lying and that I didn't want to come back to her in London? Would she think that I met someone else? Me and Joyce had plans to get married. She had suggested we get married and I had agreed. She was more than the love of my life. She was also my best friend.

I couldn't believe it was actually happening to me. I was very clear in my mind that any thoughts or hope of escape were not only foolish and impossible, but thoughts of hope may end up driving me crazy with despair. There was absolutely nothing I could do to get away or escape from the country. All I could do was to carry on living one second at a time and try to keep my sadness inside of me. Nothing would be gained from anyone seeing that I'm dying inside. No one could help me in any way. It was a very bitter pill for me to swallow. But I just had to accept it. And try and be strong for the sake of my brothers and sisters. I never ever received a reply from Joyce. I never knew if she knew what happened to me, and I never knew if she ever received the letter I sent to her.

Life goes on

Over the next few days, outwardly I was calm and fine, but inside I was extremely angry and in mental and emotional pain. My siblings were all sad, stressed and confused. Abby was about 12 years old, Ifeoma was 14 years old, and Chiat was one year younger than me, aged 17 years old. Every day was difficult and strange for all of us, and they all looked up to me to show them the way forward and protect them. I tried my best to put on a brave face, but I was just as traumatised by the change in plan as they were. I decided that life goes on and

I'd never give up trying to find a way back to London. But in the meantime, I had to try and find a way to keep living. I had to keep my inner strength and confidence and composure and be a good example for my siblings.

Hair cut

A few days after I'd been told that me and my siblings are being forced to stay, I woke up one morning to hear screaming and crying. I rushed outside to find out what was happening. I saw my sister Ifeoma trying to fight off Ma' Peter who was doing a bad butchers job of cutting Ifeoma's hair.

Ma'Peter said to Ifeoma, "Shut up and keep quiet. You think you're too good for us here with your long London hair? If you don't be quiet I'll slap you so hard you will smell yourself!".

Ifeoma's hair was long, luscious and straight. My mother used hot tongs on her hair almost daily in London to keep both of my sisters' hair straight. It broke my heart to see such a bad cutting job being done on her hair, and I didn't understand why Ma'Peter was being so cruel. My sisters were deeply proud of their hair, and I knew that this was a brutal and physically painful humiliation for her. Angrily, I intervened and said, "Are you on drugs? Leave Ifeoma alone! She doesn't deserve this!». Ma'Peter said, "She must have her hair short! She needs to go to school here and be bald headed like the other school girls here."

I went over to Ifeoma and pulled her away from Ma'Peter. Ifeoma was still crying and said to me, "Eddie can you please try and neaten my hair". I was shocked. Since she was a baby only my mother had taken care of Ifeoma's hair. I felt humbled and sad that she had turned to me in desperation as her only hope. Although I was really scared that I might not be able to do a good job, I tried to reassure her that I would help make her look decent. Ma'Peter said to me, "You stupid fool. Do you think you can do a better job than me? Nonsense!".

I did my best to comfort Ifeoma, and after I'd finished I took her to sit on the step outside the room I shared with my brother Chiat. I cut her hair as neat as I could. It ended up being very short. I was very nervous and worried that I might accidentally make it worse. I'd never cut anyone's hair before.

Later that night I reflected on the nightmare that was happening for me and my siblings. This was really happening. What had happened with Ifeoma increased my fears and confirmed that my relatives didn't care at all about how what we thought or how we felt.

I was lying in bed looking at the ceiling in the small room that I shared with my brother Chiat. I couldn't sleep, but Chiat was asleep in a single bed a few feet away across the other side of the room. I heard a noise and turned on the light. I saw a huge rat scampering, slowly and lazily across my sleeping brother and disappear into a hole in the wall. I sighed and didn't sleep at all that night.

First visit to Enugu

My mother, Chiat, Abby, Ifeoma and me went to Enugu to visit my uncle Gab who was the eldest of children from my grandfather's second wife. My grandfather had 4 wives. We first went to the bus garage in Onitsha by taxi. Then from the bus garage in Onitsha on to Enugu, was a long hot journey without air conditioning, and the bus was packed with more people than it could safely accommodate.

When we finally arrived in Enugu, we had a long three- mile walk, each of us dragging our suitcases along the road. It seemed to me that everyone in the street was watching us in our slow, humiliating procession, dragging our suitcases almost like a religious penance. Fearing for our lives every step of the way, cars and buses nearly ran us over as there was no pavement.

We finally arrived at our destination and outside his house we we're met by Gab my uncle, and Franka his fiancé. They were planning to get married soon, and in the meantime, there were already five other people staying with them temporarily, as well as us who had come to stay there for a while. Gab was a really great guy, warm, friendly and extremely welcoming even though there is not enough room for us all to sleep. Franka his fiancé was a lovely woman who welcomed us and tried to make us feel as though we belonged there.

We had arrived very late in the night and were all very tired from the journey. I was curious about where we were all going to sleep because as far as I could tell, there were only two rooms and about 15 people. I end up sleeping in a bed with 6 other people all lined up in bed together like a tin of sardines. Next to me was a young woman who seemed to be around my age, and we seemed to like each other. My mother, who is also one of the 6 of us in the bed, sees that there is a spark of chemistry between me and the young woman.

My mother said to me, "You must leave her alone, she is your sister!". I thought to myself, she's not my sister, I've never met her before. But I knew what my mother meant and I kept my behaviour polite. The other people who were there slept on the sofa or the floor.

The next morning it took a long time for us all to get washed and dressed. Water was in short supply and we had to be patient and take turns using a half filled cold bucket of water to wash ourselves in. After we were all washed and dressed I was sitting quietly looking at one of the walls and thinking about my girlfriend Joyce who was back in London. On one of the walls in his lounge area, I saw what I thought was a huge ornament of a lizard. But suddenly it moved. It was alive!! I screamed out, "There's a lizard on the wall!" Franka and Gab laughed at me and told me not worry as the lizard won't hurt me.

As if on cue, the lizard scampered across the wall, looked for a place to position itself comfortably and settled down. It stayed there looking relaxed, bobbing its head up and down manically. Soon it was joined by another huge lizard. They both were perfectly still on the wall except they both bobbed their heads up and down manically.

I was shaking with fear and horror at seeing lizards inside someone's house. I couldn't believe that Gab and Franka were so calm and relaxed about lizards running through their house. I soon found out that lizards were everywhere on roofs, in the streets all over the place. Many large ones, and various sizes, usually about 10 to 15 centimetres long. It was just normal. Everyone had lizards running through their houses and flats.

A Goodbye

About two weeks later we were back in Onitsha. It was hot and humid as usual and I was sitting on the steps outside the room I shared with my brother Chiat. I had felt very disturbed and quite traumatised by what I'd seen of Nigeria and been really sad about the experiences I'd had so far. My mother walked up to me while I was sitting alone on the step trying to figure out what I could do. My mother said, "Son I'm going back to London, and I'm not coming back to Nigeria". I couldn't believe what she was saying. I heard the words and just couldn't speak. I looked at her and hoped that she could somehow see that this was utter madness.

I was hoping and praying that she was going to say that she's going to take me with her. I tried to keep strong and not cry. And I managed to appear as though I was fine and that I would cope. But I really felt utterly abandoned and betrayed. I know that she knew full well that I would never ever have gone to Nigeria if she hadn't lied to me and tricked me into coming. It took all my inner strength to hold myself together and not break down in tears. I didn't bother asking her why she was doing this, because I knew that it wouldn't change anything.

My mother said, "It's for the best for you and your brothers and sisters. Here's a bank book for you with 200 Naira". I looked at it and took it. I wondered how long the money would last and what would I do after it ran out. I wasn't emotionally close with my mother, as I'd spent my formative childhood years with a white foster family, and I rarely talked with my mother about anything unless I had something urgent and important to tell her that she needed to know.

Even after this devastating blow I didn't have more to say to her. It was very clear that it wasn't some kind of joke. I felt sick and as though I couldn't breathe, both at the same. This was real and I was going to be stuck in Nigeria with no way out. Me and my siblings would be just left to live or survive on our own or die. I watched her as she walked off to the end of the road and disappeared. I still just couldn't believe what was happening.

A Separation

The next day my sister Abby was sent to Kaduna. Abby had been so miserable and depressed that she did not speak to anyone in Nigeria from the moment we had arrived at Lagos airport. I wasn't told who she was going to stay with. All I knew was that Kaduna is hundreds of miles away from where we were in Onitsha. I had no idea what she would be doing in Kaduna, and no way of contacting her to find out if she was going to be ok. I was worried that Abby wouldn't be able to cope without any of us with her. But there was nothing I could do.

Ifeoma was sent to an all-girls school in Onitsha called "Queens Girls School". Apparently, it had a reputation as being a very good school. I had no idea what it would be like for her, but I felt that she would find a way to survive because she was so smart and brilliant academically. That left me and Chiat in Onitsha with nothing to do.

White suit, cream shoes

One day I decided to cheer myself up and I put on the white suit that I had brought with me from London. I also put on my favourite pair of cream shoes. My brother Chiat saw me and said “Where are you going?” I said, “I’ve got a meeting”. I didn’t have anywhere to go at all, and I felt really silly saying it. I’m sure that Chiat knew that I was just pretending. I walked up to the end of the road and walked back.

Beyond the end of the road was ‘no man’s land” for me as I didn’t know where to go or in what direction. I had no money so I couldn’t go further. I was just trying to find some kind of inspiration and foolishly hoping that someone would see me in the suit and maybe think that I was worth talking to and maybe they could help me escape back to London. Every day I thought of London and what I was missing and what I should have been doing in Art school or with my girlfriend or developing my career in London. It hurt my soul to think of London. But I couldn’t help it.

What struck me profoundly was the fact that even though everyone was the same colour as me, it seemed normal. And for most of the time I never saw any white people. Only once I went into a shop in Enugu one afternoon and I saw a white man. It was a very strange and shocking experience. He really looked to me as though he didn’t belong there. In addition, he wasn’t treated with suspicion as most black people are when we go to almost any shop in London.

I felt so relaxed and I felt like a normal human being amongst an all black population in Nigeria. In London, there was always the risk of being verbally abused or beaten up or stabbed just because of the colour I was born.

Onitsha - Pretending to have something to do

As far as I could tell, Ma'Peters food shack belonged to her. Peter her son and only child, was a very mysterious man and didn't appear to have a job, but was always well dressed. Apparently, Peter had land to sell and he occasionally took me with him to visit potential clients to sell land to. It usually amounted to Peter pretending he was a 'big shot' property manager, with him and his client drinking lots of palm wine and chewing kola nuts. Although he loved to pretend to be a serious businessman, he never sold even one plot of land throughout the time I was in Nigeria. He had two sons who seemed to be spoilt. His sons were a bit younger than my brothers Chiduve and Nnabuike, but I was upset that my brothers seemed to be outcasts and yet were supposed to be part of my Aunty Ma'Peters' family.

Chiduve was still treated very badly selling water on his head. Ma'Peter hated Chiduve because he looked like my mother. Nnabuike was still treated like a king. Apparently, Ma'Peter treated him in a special way because he looked like my dad. She had really loved my dad.

I played a lot of reggae music that had never been heard in Onitsha. Songs such as Dennis Brown's "Hold on To What You Got" and "Sitting And Watching" on my stereo cassette player. During the first few days while living in Onitsha with Peter and Ma'Peter and my siblings I had a false sense of security and thought that I'd be going back to London to collect more reggae music. I'd not brought many reggae and soul and jazzfunk music compilation cassettes because I thought I'd only be in Nigeria for a short time. Peter particularly loved hearing “Sitting And Watching”, and used to make me play it over and over repeatedly for him.

One day Chiat got an offer from a friend of Peter and decided to go to Imo state. Thus happened a few weeks after Ifeoma and Abby were sent away. I didn’t know exactly what he was going to be doing there, but I understood that he was going to be working in some kind of shop. Imo state was many hours journey from where we were in Onitsha.

While Chiat was in Imo state we only saw each other a couple of times. There was a time that me and Chiat met up in Onitsha after we hadn’t seen each other for a few months. He told me that the shop he worked in Imo state had been ambushed by armed robbers and he only luckily escaped with his life.

Peanuts and bananas, Pounded Yam and pepper soup

I never went too far from the street where I lived in Onitsha, simply because mostly I had nowhere to go and no one to meet. I’d go on my own to the market which was close to the riverside but was the size of a small town itself. I made sure that I didn’t go too far inside the market as I knew that I’d easily get lost. I strolled around and tried to mentally keep track of my path until I found a reasonably cheap place to eat. I loved the food and I ate pounded yam and pepper soup almost every day. I varied it with Garri and okra soup or Rice, plantain and moi-moi.

For snacks, I bought groundnuts and bananas. Goundnuts were peanuts without salt. I was amazed how good they tasted. Almost like a small meal in itself. Both were really cheap and I could get huge amounts of both for almost no money. I was very surprised that I didn't get diarrhoea from the massive amounts of groundnuts and bananas I ate daily.

There was a book on spirituality written by someone named Abd Ru Shin. The book was called "In The Light of Truth" and given to me by Peter while I was living in Onitsha. It was a book that Peter gave to people to try and convert them to his philosophy of life. It described how life is lived in 7 dimensions. At each dimension we die and proceed to the next level when we have developed enough spiritually. The 7th and highest level is union with God. Although I found the book incomprehensible in many parts, it gave me a sense of hope that I might be able to spiritually get myself back to London.

Chinwe and 'Working 'B' Benson'

On our second day in Onitsha we were introduced to some of the local young people who lived just a few doors away from where we were staying. At first, they were excited to meet us, but once they realised that we weren't rich they quickly lost interest in us. All except Chinwe and Working B Benson.

Me and Chinwe mostly listened to music together in his place where he lived with his mother. We drank beer and talked about women. As he lived just a few metres away from the room I shared with my brother Chiat, it was easy for me to visit Chinwe and hang out. I had nothing to do while I was in Onitsha, so I visited him often. One of our favourite songs we played over and over was, 'Tonight is the night" by Betty Wright. We reminisced about the women we had loved and the women who we had lost. My heart was always with Joyce to the point where I had to eventually drop from playing the song.

Chinwe introduced me to another guy who was a year younger than me who seemed about 10 years older. He liked to call himself 'Working B Benson' because he was a working man and he smoked Benson and Hedges cigarettes. Me and Chinwe and Working B Benson spent a lot of late night evenings sitting on the steps outside of the room I shared with my brother Chiat. They loved asking me questions about life in London while I played music at a low volume on my stereo cassette player. One of their favourite songs was a jazz funk tune called "London Town" by Light Of The World ". The lyrics of the chorus of the song was, 'I wanna party in London Town'.

They loved the lyric because they wanted to go and party in London. It was a bittersweet lyric for me because I wanted to party in London too, but permanently as my home. The irony of the lyrics wasn't lost on me.

The Fela Kuti song "Beasts of No Nation" was the first Nigerian music that I bought whilst in Nigeria in Onitsha. It was on one of his albums on cassette. I often played it on my stereo, while sitting on the steps outside of the room I shared with my brother Chiat. The price for cassettes was really cheap, even by Nigerian standards. Also in those days, you could go to a record shack and choose a list of songs that you wanted and they would compile a cassette of your requests for you.

Enugu - "Thunder only happens when it's raining".

After Chiat had gone to work in Imo state, I decided to go to Enugu and stay with my uncle Gab. One morning I packed my suitcase and just left Onitsha without saying a word to

Ma' peter or her son Peter. My younger brothers were out doing errands for Ma'Peter, so I didn't have a chance to say goodbye to them before I left for Enugu. I was really sad that I couldn't do anything for them. I took a taxi for the long seven-hour journey to Gab's place in Enugu. Gab lived in an area of Enugu called Achara Layout.

The streets were laid out in a neat grid style of about 500 houses. The roads were all dusty red, but with pot holes and ditches so large that cars and sometimes buses got stuck in them. Gab welcomed me with open arms, and didn't ask me how long I was going to stay, despite me not warning him in advance that I was coming to stay with him.

Washing with a bucket in cold water in Onitsha was a communal experience. The bathing area was a semi closed alley with a wall where we used to take turns to shower in the open using a bucket. Men and women from the nearby flats and houses would all take turns in small groups early in the morning. In Enugu washing was using buckets of water in a room specially dedicated to washing.

The first time I experienced heavy rain in Enugu, I truly thought that the world was going to end. The sky was totally blacked out. It became even darker than night-time and much more menacing as there was continual, extraordinarily loud thunder. There were moments in that kind of rain and thunder where I was sure that the world was ending. I was really terrified and amazed that people seemed so calm and relaxed about it.

The thunder and lightning could last for many days and felt to me as though Armageddon had arrived. Some people actually laughed and clapped and sang and celebrated when it rained. People put out pots and pans and anything else they could find to catch the rain.

Water, was quite expensive and only came once a week, or sometimes once every two weeks in a rusty coloured van. One day I had followed a group of people I didn't know very well into a car on a mystery trip. The person I knew best was an artist named Chike. He was really talented and had a great sense of humour. We ended up in a place that had lots of tents and people were just chatting with each other in the field. Suddenly it began to rain!

Everyone ran into the nearest tent and found whatever they could to sit on and get as comfortable and keep as dry as possible. Someone had some music playing. I heard the song " Dreams" by Fleetwood Mac. I'll never forget one of the lyrics in the song that said 'thunder only happens when it's raining'. It was an eerily appropriate song while we were waiting for the rain and thunder to stop.

I had brought a copy of the book "Roots" written by Alex Haley. It had been made into a spectacularly successful TV series in America in the 1970s. I saw it on TV in the UK when I was about 14 years old. At that time in the UK in the 1970s it was unheard of for people of African-Caribbean heritage to be on TV. Everyone, even the white population watched "Roots" every week. I was listening to Herb Alpert song "Rise" over and over while reading "Roots". The irony of my situation was very clear to me!

Michael Jackson's song "Billie Jean", was a spectacular sensation throughout the whole of Nigeria at that time. It had a sadly poignant side to the song for me because it just reminded me I wasn't in London. I was trapped in Enugu watching the music video with Gab and neighbours and family and other friends. They played the video regularly on the TV, which was a pleasant surprise because in those days there were no music video channels in Nigeria.

My uncle Gab always had interesting friends who visited him in Enugu. Gab worked at a petrol station and he was a very popular man. One of his friends was a guy named Amechi who had recently returned to Enugu after years living in America. He was a few years older than me, but he had an air if someone who was very wise and experienced in life. He told many fascinating stories about his life in America, and I dreamed and hoped that Amechi might be able to help me find a way to get back to London.

I went to visit Amechi at his place a few times. He lived walking distance from Gab's place in Enugu, so it was a great and easy place to go for a change of scene when I was in Enugu. Michael Jackson's song "Human Nature", was a song I played it over and over on the record player at Amechi's house, while smoking cigarettes and drinking beer. It haunted me at night with its sad strings. Amechi loved the song too, but I was surprised that he didn't mind me playing the song repeatedly. In Enugu, Amechi visited Gab's place often while I was living with gab in Enugu.

Me and Amechi became good friends. One evening me and Gab and several other adults were drinking beer and chatting in Gabs flat. The topic of cars came up and Amechi said the greatest car he's ever seen and driven was the Volvo 760. We all laughed and joked about the merits of our favourite cars. I couldn't drive, but for months afterwards I had dreams about owning a Volvo 760 car.

In the taxi to nowhere

One day when I was running really low on money, I decided to take a desperate chance and go and see a family friend in a part of Enugu that was an office and business area. Apparently, the family friend was a big-time lawyer, and my grand plan was to beg him for some money. He was the same family friend whose house we'd stayed in when we arrived in Lagos from London. He was from Umuleri like my mother and father and he was another friend of my dead father.

It took me about 2 hours to get there walking in the hot sun, but I had to save every bit of money I had. I arrived at his office and said what my name is and was asked to wait outside because I didn't have an appointment. I waited for over 2 hours until he finally came out and invited me into his office.

He first of all spent time flattering me for who my dead father was and spent some more time telling me about the value of hard work. Before I had a chance to ask him for help he told me that he couldn't help me and that I needed to find a way to stand on my own two feet. He wished me good luck and then led me to the door. I left his office almost in tears as I thought that he could have helped me a little bit if he wanted to. But it just seemed as though he wanted to humiliate me. I decided that I wasn't going to walk the 5 miles home and got a taxi.

When I was riding around in the taxi I was down to my last few Naira and on the radio in the taxi I heard a Barry White song called – "I Wanna Lay Down Wit Ya Babe". Looking out of the windows in the taxi, the sun was going down and it was early evening. I dreamed of being back in London in the arms of my girlfriend Joyce, and lying down with her. I'd never ever heard that song before and as the song played I was lost between thoughts of complete, utter poverty and uplifting romantic music playing in the taxi.

I listened to Herb Alpert 'Fandango' album, especially the song 'Rise'in Enugu while living with Gab. Ironically reading "Roots" by Alex Hailey.

I met a disabled guy named "Ochi" in Enugu. He often talked about a part of Enugu called New Haven and he had some friends who lived there. He told me that in New Haven a lot of the houses had running water. This was a shock to me as up until then no house I'd been to had running water and it seemed as though no one in Enugu had running water.

Electricity was also a problem for everyone. Power could go off at any time and the power-cut could last for hours or days. New Haven sounded to me like paradise or even 'Heaven'. Maybe they called it New Haven because it was really heaven. I had dreams about the place being an area of love, harmony and sunshine. And I thought that maybe the people who lived there had good jobs and were well connected and maybe someone who lived there could help me get back to London. I always fantasized about going back to London. Despite my circumstances being hopeless, I never gave up on that dream.

Me and 'Ochi' never got tired of talking about and discussing and analysing our favourite film, which was "A Star is Born" – starring Barbra Streisand and Kris Kristofferson. At that time both of us had each watched the movie more than 5 times. Around that time, I often played "Electric Boogaloo " by Marcia Griffiths. Even then I thought that it was amazing that Marcia had moved away from singing reggae with Bob Marley and into the new hip hop music scene. 'Ochi' couldn't walk and had to drag himself around with the use of two hospital sticks. One for each arm. Subsequently his arms were thick and strong.

He never complained about his disability despite the fact that where he lived was particularly difficult and treacherous to walk because of numerous large potholes and ditches around the houses and streets.

He always had a girlfriend, sometimes two. He was a very charismatic guy and often when I visited him, there would be a different woman with him. I used to love visiting 'Ochi' because he was always so positive about life and he made me forget about my situation for the times that I was with him. He spoke perfect English and preferred to speak English with me, which was a relief for me because most people preferred to talk in Igbo.

We also had in common one of our favourite American soul songs by a group called The System. The song we loved by them was, "This Is for You", which I played on my music system which I brought with me when I went to visit him.

Not being able to speak the Igbo language and thus not knowing what people were saying, often left me out of conversations. When I was around people of my own age they tried to speak in English or pigeon English in order to include me. But mostly people would quickly fall into their natural Igbo language. That was really frustrating and a constant daily reminder that I was a stranger and outsider.

I always expected some people, or at least someone to ask me what I was doing in Nigeria, or why did I come to Nigeria. But no one ever did. Nobody cared. I think that initially in my first 2 weeks of being in Nigeria, I had an over estimated sense of the importance of me being born in London and having grown up in London.

But people were much more impressed with anyone who had lived or studied in America.

Once I was out at the market in Enugu with my uncle Gab. We browsed over the record section and he saw that a particular LP had caught my eye. It was the album 'Here My Dear' by Marvin Gaye. I was attracted to the artwork because the picture on the cover looked so much like my uncle Ekwelli. My dead father and Ekwelli had the same father. My father and Ma'Peter and Ekwelli were the children of my grandfather's first wife.

The Marvin Gaye album contained a song called "Sparrow" which I played over and over . It fully encapsulated my sadness, it was about a sparrow that couldn't sing because it was heartbroken. I felt like a sparrow that could no longer sing. I played that song almost throughout the time I was living with Gab in Enugu.

Fidelis Okoye

My first meeting with Fidelis Okoye was in the town of *Umuleri. Me and my mother had gone to visit him before she abandoned me and my siblings in Nigeria and went back to London. One of the first things he said to me was that my father had been poisoned through witchcraft. Echoing what my mother had told me about my father's death when I was aged 13 years old.

Umuleri and the Ancient Egyptians

*Umuleri is the Igbo town where my mother and father were from, close to the market town of Onitsha. The origin of the Igbo begins with the story of the ancestor whose name was Eri. By archaeological account, in around 2345 BC in Ancient Egypt / Kemit, a certain "M-Eru-ka (or Eru/Eri)" became a high priest to Pharaoh Teti.

From them came the sacred ancestors who founded the Igbos. Subsequently, M-Eru-ka left Ancient Egypt / Kemit with many of his family and followers and set forth towards the south-west.

The main Eri group continued until the joining point of the Rivers Niger and Anambra known as "Ezu-na-Omambala", and where it settled and founded the Agulu-Eri community near the current town of Umuleri / Agulu Eri. Eri as he was later called, entered into the territory that was to become modern Nigeria. He set up many lodges across the land, wherein Kemitian Muur Sciences were studied and practised. Some elements of those sciences and wisdom still survive in Nigeria today.

Some Ancient Egyptian words which survive in the Igbo language are as follows:

ANCIENT EGYPTIAN / IGBO (Onitsha and Uburu dialects used)

Beka (pray/confess) | Biko/Beko (to plead, please) the scents,

Budo (dwelling place) | Obodo/ubudo (country, dwelling place)

Dudu (black image of Osiris) | Mmadu (person) sights,

Amu (children) | Umu (children)

Ani (ground land below) | Ani (ground land below)

Ka (higher) | Ka (greater, higher, stronger, above) sounds,

Isi (leader) | Isi (leader, head (body part), female name as in igbo: "Isioma")

Oni (Ancient Egyptian City) | Oni-tsha (Igbo City)

Ikhenaten (name of a Pharaoh) | Ikh-em (Igbo name for a male representing high power) taste

Miri (water) | Miri (water)

Ehn/Hen (yes, nod head) | Eh (yes, nod head)

W (they) | Uwe (they, them)

The Village

Ocassionally, I went to the village of Nneyi, which is in the town of Umuleri. My father and mother were both born there. I visited my father's grave which was right beside my grandfather's grave outside my grandfather's house in Nneyi. I felt a sense of oneness with nature in the village. Life was very simple and most of the land was unoccupied. The part of the village I stayed in was close to the Anambra river. There was only one road through the town of Umuleri. That road divided the towns of Umuleri and Aguleri.

My uncle Gab had a simple small bungalow that I used to stay in when I was there. It was isolated and surrounded by land. I played music by the group 'Aswad', in particular the album 'A New Chapter Of Dub'. On my own in the fields, I contemplated my life and how I ended up in Nigeria in such unplanned and unprepared circumstances.

Sometimes I met some of the young people I knew from Onitsha who came down to the village once in a while. I went to a party in the neighbouring town of Aguleri with some friends from Onitsha when they were in Umuleri. I was anxious and concerned, because of my mother's warning of the Aguleri people's aim to destroy or kill Umuleri people by poisoning or other means.

The Anambra State House of Assembly in Enugu

It was Fidelis Okoye, who gave me a job in the local government in Enugu, as a favour to my mother. Fidelis was from Umuleri, the same as my mother and father were from Umuleri. He was a well-connected friend of my late father. Working with Fidelis was an odd experience. I sat daily in his luxurious and spacious government office and had my own desk. There were only 2 desks, mine and his. Comfortable large sofas were in the middle of the room. He never set me any work to do and was never in the office with me. I had no portfolio of work but my job title was Legislative Assistant. I loved the title, even though I knew nothing of the law!

I used to read novels and didn't even need to make the pretence of doing any work. One day Fidelis came into his office and saw me reading a novel. I tried to quickly put it away but he just said, "That's fine, carry on". I carried on reading, but I still felt uncomfortable for a while. One of the novels I chose from the collection in his office was "Fools Die" by Mario Puzo who also wrote "The Godfather".

Once a month I would take the short walk over to the payroll office and tell them who I worked for, and my name, and queue up in line to get my pay. When I mentioned that I work for Fidelis Okoye, gasps went around the payroll room and everyone treated me as though I was some kind of celebrity. I acted innocently as though I was not aware he was a powerful man. I couldn't help myself in briefly enjoying the admiration of me, but inside I laughed, as I knew it was all part of the corruption that was normal Nigerian politics.

I never knew exactly what Fidelis Okoye did, and I never asked him. He gave me the impression that it was better that I didn't know exactly what he did.

Every day I dressed as smart as I could and when I passed the security guards each morning, I tried to pretend that I was doing important work with Fidelis Okoye. Occasionally, he sent me to collect money from the bank for him in his chauffer driven Mercedes. I was amazed and shocked at how it went. I'd get in his car, sit in the back and pretend that I was some kind of dignitary.

The driver treated me as though I was a prince. The driver would take me to the bank and I'd wait for him in the car while he' d go in the bank and come out a while later with a briefcase which he'd give to me. Then we'd drive back to the Anambra State House of Assembly and I'd go into the office and give the briefcase to Fidelis Okoye. I did that maybe once a month. I loved the job, and it was a little bit of paradise for me.

The House of Assembly was a very impressive imposing building with a lot of stone stairs before you reached the entrance. It was situated in beautiful grounds with carefully cut and well maintained grass all around the building. In front were fountains with golden basins. On tall poles, also in front of the building were flags of many countries of the world. It looked a bit like a United Nation's building.

I was never fully relaxed or complacent about my pretend job working with Fidelis Okoye and sure enough without any warning, after about 4 months it was over and I was out of a job due to the local government running out of money. My little dream world ended, and I was back down to earth with no new way to survive. I had been very prudent with the money I'd earned, and I hardly spent any of it. I had only used just the bare minimum daily to keep me alive, as I knew that I couldn't be sure where my next money was going to come from.

Chief Mazi Mperempeh Entertainment group

I tried to learn Igbo, but I just couldn't do it. I felt terrible being outcast due to not being able to speak the Igbo language. I tried hard to learn words and phrases when people were talking, but it's really hard to learn a language unless you're having structured teaching. So, I went to a local college. Initially I went there just out of curiosity and as something to do. I hung around in the canteen and enjoyed the cheap student food.

One day while I was in the college canteen I saw a guy I knew from London. He was sitting at a table surrounded by a large group of women and they were all laughing and joking. We immediately recognised each other and I was embarrassed because I didn't know what I was going to say about how and why I was in Nigeria. He spoke first and said he'd been forced to stay in Nigeria by his parents because he was bad in London. He'd been in Nigeria for some years and he was studying at the college. I felt helpless and lost hope even more.

The fact that he had been in Nigeria for years made me think there really was no hope of me ever returning back to London. Humiliatingly, I told him that I was in a similar situation, but actually worse, because I didn't know why I had been tricked into coming to Nigeria, and there had been no plan for what I would do in Nigeria. He told me that one of the best things I could do for myself is to learn the language, and that there are Igbo classes in the college. He was studying Mass Communications. We parted and promised to keep in touch.

A few weeks later I was at the college just to go and hang out in the college canteen.

Before I got there, I heard laughter and clapping and I initially thought that the guy I had known in London was becoming really fantastically popular. But when I got to the canteen there was a very short man speaking in 'Pidgeon English doing a brief comedy show in the college cafe area. His name was Mazi Mperempeh. I'd never heard of him but he was a well know comedy performer from Lagos.

He regularly toured around colleges in the country, putting on performances, and looking for talent to join his company. At the end of his performance I went up to him to congratulate his show. He heard my accent, asked me where I'm from and invited me to come to a rehearsal with his group. A few days later I went to meet him and his group in an old warehouse in Enugu and signed up immediately to be part of his company.

Theatre group membership cards were given out to all members and we had to pay a membership fee. It was a small company with a performance team of about 15 people. As a result, they were always looking for new members, but new performers were hard to find. For a while I was concerned that it might be part of a money- making scam, but it quickly became apparent that he was genuine because occasionally when I was at home with Gab, I saw some of the commercial advertisements on Nigerian television that Mazi Mperempeh had made for companies.

I went on to do some very small theatre shows where I was a dancer in a group of male and female dancers. I did some comedy TV, where I played the role of newsreader and we did a few radio advertisements for food and drinks companies. It was a long and difficult bus journey to go for rehearsals. Even though the bus fare was cheap, I was becoming more and more worried because I was seriously running out of money. I was never under any illusions about my acting ability. I knew that I was the news reader because I had the best English accent.

But also, they were very short of men, so I was a much needed addition to the group. I thought to myself 'why not? I've nothing else to do'. The theatre / dance show we did was dancing to Michael Jackson's song – "Wanna be starting something" (I thought he was singing 'we've got a son'!) The costumes we wore were red tops, blouse like wit frilly sleeves, black trousers and black shoes.

They all loved my dancing, especially my spins! The members would all clap and cheer when I danced. I never thought that I was actually all that good a dancer.

At Gabs place, sometimes occasionally I saw Charlie and Tony when they came to visit Gab in Enugu, both were really great guys. They were Gabs' brothers. Tony was about the same age as me and Charlie was some years older. They were the children of my grandfather's second wife. My grandfather had 4 wives and a lot of children. I met 3 of the wives and a lot of the children when I went to visit the village. When my father was alive, he only had one wife, even though he could have had more wives if he wanted to, as Nigeria is a polygamous society.

A celebrity in Ajassa Street

From time to time I would go to Onitsha for a change of scene. I had nothing to do there and I'd stay just a few days at the room I'd originally shared with my brother Chiat. It amazed me that Ma'Peter never asked how I was surviving and never questioned what I was doing for a living with my life. She also never asked me how long I was staying for. I lived so much on instinct and intuition that I would just wake up and go back to Enugu or stay in Onitsha, purely based on how I felt when I woke up in the morning. Nothing mattered anyway. I had no place I ever needed to be.

I had an ear-ring in my left ear. It was a small golden hoop ear-ring which I loved wearing. But at that time in Onitsha it was almost unheard of for a man to wear an ear-ring. Children would run up to me in the street laughing and clapping. Someone had seen me and told their friends and word spread so that sometimes crowds of children would be laughing and clapping in Ajassa Street when they saw me.

In addition, people had seen me on the TV acting in the comedy shows with Mazi Mperempeh Entertainment Group. It seemed that I was a celebrity. But only on Ajassa street. To the wider community I remained unknown and anonymous. I was glad for that because I had virtually no money and could not pretend to be living a celebrity life.

"The taste of the pudding is in the eating!"

There came a time when me and my uncle Gab started to not get on well with each other. I ended up moving out and going to live with a group of journalists on a hill in a semi isolated area of Enugu. One of the people who used to drink with us was a wealthy man who often used to by drinks for all of us who were there whenever he came in for a drink in Ochefu's shack. He spent most of the time complaining about his two wives. I always felt that having married the two wives he knew what he was in for. There were some soldiers who I used to drink beer with, including Ben, who was a close friend and neighbour of my uncle Gab. Me and Ben had struck up a great rapport soon after I moved to live in Enugu. Gab had introduced me to him.

I did virtually nothing while I was living with the small group of journalists. We talked politics all the time during the day, or drinking at night at Ochefu's bar with soldiers. The soldiers who hung out in Ochefu's shack, usually got really drunk and rowdy, and would often order drinks for everyone else in the bar. Often, they would order a crate load of 24 bottles at a time and invite whoever was nearby to come and join them.

Once there was a heated debate going on in Ochefu's beer shack. It was a packed night and the soldiers had been buying everyone drinks. Most people were drunk.

Including me. The wealthy man with two wives tried to make a point about how you know if a woman is right for you. He was trying to say to one of the soldiers that you only know what something is like when you try it. He said "The taste of the pudding is in the eating!" For some unknown reason the whole bar joined in and shouted in unison "The taste of the pudding is in the eating!" repeatedly for a few minutes until we all fell about drunk and laughing.

From that moment on, everyone would say the taste of the pudding is in the eating as the answer to any discussion!

Meeting Ojukwu with Journalists I lived with

The place I lived in with the journalists, was up a hill with an amazing view of the houses nearby and below us. A surprisingly beautiful area, but because it was isolated from the main road it was very cheap.

C.Don Adinuba, an experienced journalist, had studied at Howard University in America. He had only one eye but nobody ever said anything about it. He was fanatical about politics and very knowledgeable about the world. I was surprised that he was back in Nigeria and wondered what had brought him back to Nigeria from America. But I never asked him. While I lived with them we endlessly discussed the merits of Chinua Achebe' s writing compared to Wole Soyinka' s writing. It was a conversation that we carried on each day, picking up from wherever we left off from the night before. We also talked a lot about politics in Nigeria and the rest of the world. They gave me a good African political education.

Nnamdi Jonson was also an experienced journalist who was very much in awe of the writer Wole Soyinka and also in awe of the former politician named Emeka Ojukwu. who was his political hero. Chukwuemeka "Emeka" Odumegwu Ojukwu was a former Nigerian military officer and politician who served as the military governor of the Eastern Region of Nigeria in 1966 and the leader / President of the breakaway Republic of Biafra from 1967 to 1970. Biafra, was an Igbo country in West Africa which existed only from 30 May 1967 to January 1970. The capital of Biafra was ENUGU where I lived.

Biafra's declaration of independence from Nigeria resulted in civil war between Biafra and the rest of Nigeria. Biafra was officially recognised as an independent country by Gabon, Haiti, Ivory Coast, Tanzania and Zambia.

Nations, which did not give official recognition but provided support and assistance to Biafraincluded Israel, France, Spain, Portugal, Norway, Rhodesia, South Africa and Vatican City.

Biafra also received aid from non-government organisations, including Joint Church Aid, Holy Ghost Fathers of Ireland, and under their direction Caritas International, and U.S.

Catholic Relief Services. Médecins Sans Frontières (Doctors Without Borders) also acted in response to the suffering.

John Lennon (of The Beatles) returned his M.B.E to the Queen in protest because he was sick and disgusted at what was being done to the Igbo people by the British Government. Most of the inhabitants of Biafra were Igbo, who led the secession due to economic, ethnic, cultural and religious tensions among the various peoples of Nigeria.

After two-and-a-half years of war, almost two million Biafran civilians died from starvation caused by the total blockade of the region by the rest of Nigeria and the British Government. Biafran forces surrendered to the Nigerian Federal Military Government in 1970.

After he'd been living outside of Nigeria for 13 years in exile, the Federal Government of Nigeria under President Shehu Shagari granted an official pardon to Emeka Odumegwu-Ojukwu and opened the road for his triumphant return to Nigeria in 1982. And that's when I met him. The entire Igbo nation took to calling him Dikedioramma ("beloved hero of the masses") during the time of him living in his family home in Nnewi, Anambra State.

C.Don Adinuba and Nnamdi Jonson were really excited about a speech that was going to be given by Emeka Ojukwu in the Igbo village that Ojukwu was from. We travelled by car to the village of Nnewi where Emeka Ojukwu lived. It was already dark and late in the evening by the time we got there. A large crowd that was surprisingly quiet in anticipation of the great Igbo liberator and leader, waited expectantly. It was almost like a religious gathering.

Finally he arrived, and when he stood on a stage with the light shining on him, he appeared to be floating. Unfortunately for me I couldn't understand a word he said because he spoke purely in Igbo. Despite my not understanding what he'd said, I still felt a tremendous feeling of upliftment and on the journey home we all were silent, lost in our own thoughts.

The Miracle return to London

It was about 16 months after I'd been trapped in Nigeria and I was living with a group of journalists in an isolated part of Enugu. I had no money at all, and the journalists that I was living with were so broke that when we showered we had to use the soap powder used for washing clothes. One morning I'd just had a shower and I was standing on the balcony of the flat I shared with the journalists. I was really at my wits end. I felt that there was no way that I could survive another day.

I had absolutely no money at all and I didn't feel I could ask any of the journalists who I was living with for money. I always put a brave face on my situation even though I was really worried. I couldn't see how I was going to survive for one more hour, and certainly I could not survive for one more day. I felt I had reached the end of my life. There was nothing I could do and no one else to turn to. It was the end. There was no way out.

I thought that my death was going to be humiliating and embarrassing as a beggar on the street. I felt that I wished that I could have a quick death and not have to suffer the shame and embarrassment of being from London but a failure. I was going to have to face up to the fact that I was going to die of hunger and starvation. I remember looking at the sky and I said in my mind "God help me ".

At exactly that moment, far away in the distance I saw a figure walking towards the flat where I was still standing with a towel wrapped around my waist. No one ever came to where we were living as it was so isolated. Even though I couldn't yet see who the person was, I went from the balcony into the lounge and announced to the journalists, "I'm going back to London!". It turned out that the person who was walking to the flat was my mother! I don't know how or why, but I felt that something inside me knew she had come to take me back to London. For me, it was a miracle.

From 1977 to 1983, Chiduve and Nnabuike lived in Nigeria for 5 years. Me, Chiat, Ifeoma and Abi had been in Nigeria for 16 months. My mum came to Nigeria and went around the country to find all of us and bring us back to London with her. We had to sneak out of the country and she told Ma'Peter and her son Peter a cover story so that they wouldn't know she was taking us all back to London.

Re- union with Joyce

In November 1983 it was winter, but not yet freezing cold winter, when I returned to London. Driving in a taxi from Heathrow airport to Battersea, with all my brothers and sitters for the first time together in 6 years, was a deeply surreal experience. The very first thing that struck me was that everything seemed so quiet and all the cars seemed brand new. It took me a while to understand, because most of the cars that I saw in Nigeria were old, smashed up and battered. In addition, drivers in Nigeria used their car horns at full blast constantly.

On arriving home in Battersea, the first thing I did was get to a phone and call Joyce. She burst into tears immediately, and could hardly speak for a while due to so many tears. I couldn't believe that I was really back in London talking with her on the phone. I was a realist and knew that anything could have happened and she could have met someone else. But talking to Joyce was better than I hoped and dreamed of.

We met up the very next day immediately and got back into a relationship together. She looked more beautiful than my memory. She was the wind through my tree. She moved me. I had forgotten how much I loved the way she smelled. She told me that in all the time that I had been in Nigeria she had never dated anyone else. I don't know how long she would have stayed single but I was secretly hoping that she had been waiting for me.

There was an intense, spiritually deep understanding, as we finally saw each other again. At first very few words were said. She intuitively knew that there was a lot for us to talk about, but only at the right time. We just looked into each other's eyes and knew we were back together.

After losing Joyce and finally getting back with her, I decided to always count my blessings and never look to the past about things that can't be changed. I was overjoyed to be in London, and looking forward to beginning a new life with Joyce.

LESSONS LEARNED FROM MY EXPERIENCE IN NIGERIA

I developed my attitude of not getting angry about things you can do nothing about.

I learnt to live the best you can be, from moment to moment. Not even one day at a time.

My attitude to running water and electricity changed. I never took it for granted

I try to never let a tap run with water just wasting.

I learnt to count my blessings and always look for the positives in life.

Our Attitude To Life Determines Our Experience